I STUDIED ONCE AT
A WONDERFUL FACULTY

Tua Forsström was born in 1947 in Borgå and lives in Tenala, Finland. A much acclaimed Finland-Swedish poet, she has won major literary honours in Sweden as well as Finland. She published her first book in 1972, *En dikt om kärlek och annat* (A Poem About Love and Other Things), followed by *Där anteckningarna slutar* (Where the Notes End, 1974), *Egentligen är vi mycket lyckliga* (Actually We Are Very Happy, 1976), *Tallört* (Yellow Bird's-nest, 1979), and *September* (September, 1983).

Tua Forsström achieved wider recognition with her sixth collection, *Snöleopard* (Snow Leopard, 1987), notably in Sweden and in Britain, where David McDuff's translation (Bloodaxe Books, 1990) received a Poetry Book Society Translation Award. *Marianergraven* (The Mariana Trench, 1990) was followed by *Parkerna* (The Parks, 1992), which won the Swedish Academy's Finland Prize and was nominated for both the major Swedish literary award, the August Prize (rare for a Finland-Swedish writer) and for Finland's major literary award, the Finlandia Prize (now given only for prose). *Efter att ha tillbringat en natt bland hästar* (After Spending a Night Among Horses) appeared in 1998. She won the Swedish Academy's Bellman Prize in 2003.

In 2003 she published her trilogy, *Jag studerade en gång vid en underbar fakultet* (I studied once at a wonderful faculty), whose English translation by David McDuff and Stina Katchadourian was published by Bloodaxe Books in 2006. This combines her three collections *Snow Leopard*, *The Parks* and *After Spending a Night Among Horses* with a new sequence, *Minerals*.

Other awards given to Tua Forsström include the Edith Södergran Prize (1991), Pro-Finlandia Medal (1991), *Göteborgs-Posten*'s poetry prize (1992), Gerald Bonnier poetry prize (1993), Tollander Prize (1998) and Nordic Council Literature Prize (1998). She has also been nominated for the European Aresteion Prize. Her poetry has been translated into several languages, including Finnish, Danish, Dutch, French, Spanish and English.

TUA FORSSTRÖM

I studied once at a wonderful faculty

translated by
DAVID McDUFF
& STINA KATCHADOURIAN

BLOODAXE BOOKS

ISBN: 1 85224 649 9

First published 2006 by
Bloodaxe Books Ltd,
Highgreen,
Tarset,
Northumberland NE48 1RP.

www.bloodaxebooks.com
For further information about Bloodaxe titles
please visit our website or write to
the above address for a catalogue.

Bloodaxe Books Ltd acknowledges
the financial assistance of
Arts Council England, North East.

Cover printing by J. Thomson Colour Printers Ltd, Glasgow.

Printed in Great Britain by
Bell & Bain Limited, Glasgow, Scotland.

CONTENTS

ACKNOWLEDGEMENTS

I studied once at a wonderful faculty was first published in Swedish as *Jag studerade en gång vid en underbar fakultet* by Söderströms (Helsinki) in 2003. It includes three books previously published by Söderströms: *Snow Leopard* (*Snöleopard*), 1987, *The Parks* (*Parkerna*), 1992, and *After Spending a Night Among Horses* (*Efter att ha tillbringat en natt bland hästar*), 1998, together with a new sequence, *Minerals* (*Mineraler*). David McDuff's translation of *Snow Leopard* was first published by Bloodaxe Books in 1990.

Some of these translations first appeared in *Books from Finland*, *Scandinavian Review* and *Stand*.

Thanks are due to FILI (Finnish Literature Information Centre), Helsinki, for translation grants awarded to David McDuff and Stina Katchadourian. Special thanks are also due to Iris Schwanck and Marianne Bargum for their help.

Snow Leopard

(1987)

translated by
DAVID McDUFF

One never swims out into the same water
In the light night waits immediately below
One falls like a leaf through the space
of seconds, a wind blows
darkness against your cheek.

I

There is a certain kind of loss
and September's objectivity

Something is released imperceptibly,
and is displaced: it does not

matter. There is a coolness
that has settled on the surfaces,

it kept me calm. One sits
on a bench that looks like other benches,

trains leave on time, dogs bark,
one is. Near you

I read books and confused my name
with names of other places: a summer kitchen

with radio news for blowing curtains,
the cousin sailing in the bay

I stood on the threshold of my mother's
bedroom, she was not there

Bedrooms smell different in summer:
a weather of gentle snowfalls

One sees a snake and treads carefully
on the grass for a few days   Still weakened

by revenge: I inform against myself. There was
a magic room called Childhood

and always the same alien particulars
For a long time I kept calm. And now

the wind takes hold of the sail
and drives my cousin straight across the bay

The small red sail red against the green

Foliage mirrored in the eye, the broken neck
describes what it's like to be a bird and fly
towards foliage mirrored in the shiny heavens:
a confused memory of the joy in rushing
to one's encounter with someone so like oneself.

In the photographs your
eyes are a shade
asymmetrical, there is
no formula for human beings. Water
and light strangely distributed
Infractions, imagination.
Nakedness. Innocence and crime.
The rondo flows from one of the
inner rooms: something completed
and inevitable
'In order to be able to live in the world
one must first lay its foundation'
I slit open an envelope
with a knife, freshly mown grass
steams in through the window
It's the suddenness!
In slow processes!
I say that I regret it all
I regret it almost all, it
makes no difference
I knew you since I was a
child and thought like a child
Yes, water and light.
Cracks in the socle.
Inflammations.

Juvena Skin Concentrate
on face and throat.
There is something that is preparing
its departure, fussing with foreign
currency, mumblingly trying
to attract attention.
But everything's all right, I say!
Over the pines in the west the sky is on fire.
Juvena Hydroactive Care
on temples and throat.

It is the way it is.
It may seem
hopeless.
It is hopeless.
Act only according
to the instructions, avoid
hysteria. Avoid
anorexia nervosa. At first
one cries a lot, doesn't want
to be a mistake and the Flowers of
Evil. One begins to feel better.
Someone stretched out
naked and didn't want to.
Someone let it happen.
One acknowledges receipt of parcels
that contain darkness quarried
from darkness in another place.
One reports oneself missing.
One reports oneself injured.
I held someone tightly
in my mouth until it
flowed over.

It was like pouring water over a peacock.
Wandering through the basement of a nightclub looking for
someone long since forgotten.
A footprint in dried clay.
An impotent mathematical formula.
It was like making an invitation to the waltz
stumbling forward on crutches.
'Foolish, Sir! Each year you stubbornly persist
in visiting this Imaginary Festival, This Vale
of Tears, These Loathsome Springs. At the last moment
you ask to postpone your departure. This
happens without fail. Without fail you sink
back into brooding about life's glowing days of
windfall. You will probably always re-
turn empty-handed. Won't you?'

Clouds of sand and litter are whirling

Perhaps some day one will emerge on the other
side, in the cool reading rooms

Someone is spilling me out like water

We request the speedy settlement of the
following matter: the house with the closed
shutters. That noise goes on all round the clock:
wailing, laughter, the sound of *Fiddler on the
Roof* and a monotonous mumbling.
We are normal, particularly ordinary people.
It sounds as though heavy objects are being dragged
across the floor. In between there is silence.
We demand silence! Identities,
particulars and a full confession:
that it be proved without delay that they are foreigners.
It is getting dark, it is still snowing, we demand
swift intervention on the council's part.

The Fieldmouse's Prayer

Father, in the blowing greenery of Your summer,
Father, in the endlessly green vault of Your summer:
Help me to get down into the ditch when Your
elect draw near along the road.

Dust swarms in the sunbeam.
On familiar terms with the Divine
you stand at the blackboard, expounding
the movements of the Soul and Love's
effect on the digestion.
You are wearing a pin-stripe suit,
you are handsome. The plainest
of the female students raises
her hand and asks in intense embarrassment
'why one doesn't faint with grief'.
You return to Descartes' *Treatise
on the Passions of the Soul*, Article XCVII.
From the corridor there is a smell of damp wool.
You look round: pupils dilated with
desire and darkness mirroring their reflection.

They come out at dusk, flat
shadows across the fields. They are composed in equal
parts of pig, badger, fox. Helplessness
is their principal distinguishing mark. They root in the snow
for something to eat. We find them unnatural:
their aimless wandering, their hunger, their obscene
lack of protection. At the first sign of danger the raccoon dog
lies down and pretends to be dead. We find such behaviour
pitiful, we find the pitiful repulsive, we
are outraged by the hungry shadows of
this sugar-beet field, so unlike the snow leopard that silently
pursues its prey six thousand metres
above sea-level.

Does one get used to them, Claes?
Those scenes of accidents?

Music is order, play
so that the subterranean parts

overwinter, all that is yearning
and prison, *Claire de Lune*

Friendship is a loneliness
freed from loneliness's fear

Does one get used to them, Claes?
Those scenes of accidents?

Months of animosity, the vapour of fever
and distance in the children's breathing

The waterfall, the unceasingly collapsing
wall of tears and interruptions

What's left is perhaps
temporary rooms, an uneventful

view of a country road in October.
Play so that something overwinters

us all and the gentle trees
in a season of cracking glass.

There is something about
the taxi-driver's boyish
cheeks that says:
that it exists.
That it really exists.
That a nocturnal music
flows along the ice-cold road.
Yes, there is a glowing point
somewhere for us all where
rags and masks will fall.
So that there will never
have been any rags or masks.
There we are eye against eye,
ashes against rain.

To live in its reflection
was sufficient. Rain

streams like silver in June
An entertainment's going on. We are

acted out on an old-fashioned open-air stage
with birch trees, in transformation

I long for home. The sense of
lightness in the water

The sense of lightness when one
comes out of the water

One asks someone to come back,
they come back at night

uninvited. Rain streams
against silver-rotting wood

There is always a bit left over

There is always a bit left over.
In the view here of green-shadowed water, reeds
shadowed by trees, the mud, the crickets...
One must have an Image to retain.
A net of gaudy fishes, a forgotten
book in the grass for the wind
to leaf through. A dancing bear.
One must hold up one's Image
against the subterranean thunder.
One must confess a Weakness:
inflamed eyes, one's love.
Those short journeys can be very long.
In the newspaper contemporaries have begun to die,
even the winters have become strangely imperceptible.
Oh what trickery, Mr Livingstone!
One writes on one's wall: 'They must show
they were fools and miserable like us'
Yes, there is a sleep that must be slept,
but first one wants to grow potatoes
and sign up for an excursion.
It takes time to learn boogie,
believe me, Sir, it takes time.
There's a wind from the west now
One must be able to reconstruct everything,
things that never happened.
O gall-sores of the soul! The heart's
blisters! Arms around shoulders, brightly dressed
friends, giggling in the late evening
on the gravel under the chestnut trees
It takes time to learn something.

In the wind a vapour of lakes and waterweed
What you saw today no one has seen
and you will remember, or forget.
But the first chord remains.

It was in the shadow of the green room
with low windows shadowed by the lime tree's foliage

in the shadow of a cloud. It was the kind of day
when animals seek out water

as we seek out springs, the pure
coolness in a loved embrace and cathedrals,

the green rooms under water shadowed
by clouds. 'It's like in physics'

says a schoolchild conducting the world's first
experiment with water, salt and sand

noting in an exercise book: 'An underwater
sandstorm whirls towards the bottom of the vessel'

and that we all consist of the same water, dance
and vertigo, and a few plain coincidences

and something that goes beyond ourselves.
I must stop here. You will certainly

have read many letters on this subject, and are tired.
One wanders from one room to the other

through the days like shadows, clouds.

II

We in embracing nights,
we fall from closeness to closeness,
and where the loving one melts,
we are a stone that plummets.

RAINER MARIA RILKE

Thank you for Your kind parcel.
I must, however, return everything:
there are plenty of scissors, stones grow
into mountains, and the chains were too heavy
even for Selma, my cow.
That's enough of the Flowers of Evil, and
this and that and another.
Mother said I was a darling child,
but she has stopped crying.
Sometimes it is spring, and sometimes it is winter.
It was brilliant night, and the farmhouse plummeted
like a falling star through space.
Fire burns more quickly than one thinks.
It's like this: there's a house somewhere,
oops! there's no house anywhere.
I have seen a photograph of the University.
But where are you at nights?
They found charred newspapers in the snow
right up at the Marsh, I miss
Father and Mother, but one has to be somewhere.
Everyone says I shouldn't have done it.
I have carpet beetles and snot in my hair,
one shouldn't get oneself in such a mess.
It's a question of being a good pupil!
A Nebula is a mist of incandescent garbage.
Before, I used to mourn both life and death, ought
I all the same to be sorry about Selma?
They bring the food in on green trays
I am terribly hungry, so I must eat instead
Mother said I fluttered like a butterfly
over the garden path, but she's not crying any more.
Mother raked the garden path beautifully.
It's not nice to eat so much.

It's nice not to be sad any more.
I dreamed that someone unbuttoned my blouse
and rusty iron bled from my mouth
onto the floor. Otherwise everything is fine.

Dear Marilyn Monroe

I read about you in the newspaper again.
You stood outside your house in Beverly Hills
and said you were the sum total of
forty lonely hotel rooms.
You were dressed in provocative attire,
even your hair was radiant as a cloud.
I myself have never stayed in a hotel.
I am writing to you because one ought to avoid
certain people, as far as possible
They need all that they see.
They need you because you are radiant
and like a child. Do you know
what people are saying about the Attorney General?
And also about the President and yourself?
I don't mean to be nosey, believe me
But I am older than you,
and not so good-looking: Between night and dawn
someone will take your life   In the morning
they will go to church with their wife and children
It's none of my business, of course
There is a lot in the newspaper about nerves
What I mean is: you are sort of precious
You are like something in us all
You constantly talk about death, but you have
never been hurled into the deep darkness that drowns
a person in night and ashes without mercy
So avoid dressing half-naked
Don't whisper that funny way when you sing
Avoid solitary walks and darkness   Your house
can hardly be seen for all the greenery in the pictures,
are you interested in gardening?

You were right: it's fine here.
What mirror-gleaming floors, reflecting
the shiny crystals in the garden!
Immediately after our arrival we were given
the task of whitewashing the frescoes,
we made it clean and tidy
Here I practise my obedience
I practise my ability to see: the disintegration of
matter, the damp, the fine
cracks, the silence, that everything rots.
If one doesn't immediately prevent it!
If one doesn't constantly putty and paint over!
I don't dare to think that thought: how I used to live
my life in the mire, like a pig!
Every day we set aside four hours for Systematisation
One soon gets used to it, you were right of course
One also gets used to the chronology
Some of my friends are regrettable exceptions
They copy from oblivion at nights
events where planets play a part, market days,
cattle auctions, the time
of the arrival of snow that lies.
The durability of darkness.
I think I ought to report them, I don't know
They talk about strange kinds of birds, and about
the word having power over people's
hearts. A curious faith
The sanitary arrangements are excellent
Another advantage is that one doesn't have to die
I really have nothing to complain of. I
have now completely forgotten the old
geography: all that was rain, membranes
of fever and salt.

III

PENELOPE

(Cantata)

1

I am Wife, besieged.
Years flowed like water,
One gets used to it. Sometimes
I would separate from my waiting
And look at my Suitors, deprived of
You. I forgot myself, I forgot
The nights under His hands
As one forgets the dream until
It recurs. Years passed
Like moments. There is
Such waiting that one separates

2

What we call time
Is perhaps to train oneself
In want, uncertainty.
What we call time
Is perhaps finally to give up!
I forget His name!
I forget how I wailed
With desire, tired in the morning light!
Now the Suitors devastate the house.
I forget! I forget
His name!
War corrupts. Memory diminishes.
To besiege or be besieged
Makes no difference in the end. But
Like spilled-out water be denied an
Embrace? Oh if I could only glimpse
Your armour in the crowd!

3

Bones hair feathers scales!
The years pass gaily and evening draws in
Inviolable are the minerals' laws caking
The earth, the gaudy surfaces are flaking:
Over the unattended face that was sleep's
Over the unattended face that was the dream's
Unattended mask

4

A body is to bear a shrine
Of relics, bones like porcelain
I am not yet an old
Woman, it distresses me!
I am weaving a web. I dreamed
Last night of a vessel drifting
Towards a far-off shore
Do you remember me? The one who
Returns is always another
With his forehead marked by war's shadow,
And his body engraved with the scars
Of all that is not his own!
Who returns as the person one was?
What one has lost is real:
What one has lost one has
And keeps forever. A waiting,
A Man. Do You remember me?
Hurry, if You can.

IV

For there is no place that does not
see you. You must change your life.

RAINER MARIA RILKE

1

Come home from those dark waters
Come home from out of the storm
Like a first-former with your red
schoolbag on your back, come
home. Confusing what
was, confusing you.
The days look like one another.
Rows of jars filled with blood and mucus.
It's a question of not remembering
It's a question of not remembering that morning
down by the shiny water, real
as an imagining!
Once there was innocence and pleasure
Once there was a reckless purity
One is a moment
One is a floor of sand in the market tent
One ferries small children and ice-skates
to and fro along slippery winter roads in one's yearning
for the cool light, come home

2

There is a despair
so great that it cannot be seen: a smoke
in our breath on cold days, a weariness,
a dream of surrender
It merges with the water's cycle
that holds our bodies captive
It occupies our memories and returns
its inventories in unrecognisable condition
Its victims oppose
rescue. Its sign is want
It lacks gestures or
written signs: shells of small creatures
stratified to limestone.

There is a despair as inescapable
as ice, the fishes' white-shimmering sky.

3

In order to destroy those we love
we dress them up as fools in the
Nocturnal Theatre. And they rise in revolt!
We stand there like clowns ourselves!
Masked into dream they were even more
themselves. Tender-footed felines. Strong,
uncorrupted. They are going to deceive us.
What we call time deceives us.
I myself for example am the sort of person
who continues to wander up and down
the short familiar stretch between high-rise blocks
with the far too difficult music in my bag and
an objective, growing despair at
being myself. It is October with metallic
air, metallic sky and the banished
loved ones who walk with us in the smoke
of our breath. We look at them,
we must never lose them again.

4

I see you in the slow night.
There is a scent of water and bird-cherry.
Hair is coming loose in drifts on the sheet,
perhaps it will regenerate itself, it doesn't
matter, but it is coming loose.
I know how to handle the simpler
firearms, it doesn't help me.
I lack sexual imagination.
One buys something in ready-made parts
and they won't fit together.
One lets oneself be covered in
mud and the nausea of Grief.
But I don't want to be among these nights'
Emergency vehicles, shapes floating across
the water-damaged mirror, the waste
from the immense slaughterhouses!
Bird-cherry blossoms in the vase, drops vermin
over the tablecloth's blue embroideries of care.
A texture falls apart.
I lack sexual imagination, the bodies
that poured the secretion of their terrible
tenderness into each other. Oh, is there
anywhere that does not see you?
The night scrapes at the skeleton.
A texture slowly falls apart:
without the hope that is memory
we would not exist.

5

As in a mirror
the light images float by:
little girls with pigtails walk here
along the garden streets, frail
old ladies. One looks round for
one's lover, that was another time.
The temperature varies here.
One converses politely:
'I'd appreciate a bit less
speed', 'If necessary I shall have to kill you'
But how is one to know what's rubbish?
What's broken and what is without flaws?
Forget everything that hurt you so much.
You are going to be tortured like a feathered
caress, you are going to be tortured to
a gall-burst fish, you are going to be tortured
to darkness dissolved in darkness.

6

The works hotel turns out to be
a nocturnal construction of rotten
wood gleaming against the black greenery
There is an odour of lakewater
and August. Not a soul
in sight
So one must sleep here
So one must read some books,
take one's medicine and sleep
Instead I dream of the face that
splits open in bleeding fissures
'You are time that must be whiled away'
A window stands barely open on the night
A window stands barely open on the morning light,
someone is raking gravel and singing *The Trout*,
in the town across the bay a bus is starting up.
And I don't know whether I have been alone.

7

Sometimes visitors
are appalled by the house's seclusion,
the green darkness under the trees.
But I do have the main road!
Itinerant companies while away
the days with merry pranks
The dead and maimed are ferried
to and fro on carts during the night
The dwarfs grin and try to
creep in under my skirts
It never gets really lonely here
As long as I have the main road!

8

As in prayer
a little girl stands still
with raised hands
in the water, swims out. So our summers
go by: in the shadow beneath tall
trees, and the other shore in sunlight.
The smoke from the sauna wanders strangely
along the slope
A mist drifts across the water:
The one you are waiting for will not arrive
The one you are waiting for is travelling elsewhere
Dew is falling, apples are falling
A girl is still playing on the shore
as if she were little
'But can't you see? It's me!'
It starts to snow violently:
We take place at unknown depths
in insufficient light, but even what
can be seen is beautiful.
The cracks, the water. Vessels
of fever and salt.

It was the hottest day of the summer.
We walked down by the water, and you
who have become my brother talked about
someone who had fallen ill, football matches,
Thelonious Monk and the factory
you had visited in your dream, familiar
and different for each person
You said that nothing is ever finished
You said that everything is transitory

except for a few glowing
and soiled pictures that are sorrow, that
are the sorrow that flows through
friendship like water,

a few over-exposed sequences that
we press ashamedly to our hearts.

The Parks

(1992)

translated by
DAVID McDUFF

We are transformed into what we love.

VERNER VON HEIDENSTAM

With lilies woven in her hair
With ears that look like ass's ears
That one tries to cleanse a wound of
rubbish and that it doesn't matter
I put the picture away and can look at it

And that we must be those people

I write to you because
I no longer think it's
dangerous to stay here after
the approach of darkness. Doors open
and close. People hurry past under
the brilliant lanterns, it's in
the nature of waiting that people should hurry past.
I waste my days here doing
nothing. In foreign cities too
we make ourselves something that looks like a home:
a street, an unpretentious block, a few ugly
houses. A view. A tree. A green
tree we pass in the rain and get attached
to without knowing its name. I don't want
you to be distorted.

We find it hard to
see clearly at high
speeds and in
darkness, those burning
moments of halogen
against halogen, I can't
pick you out. That the sun
walked alongside in the water.
An afternoon in August
in a South German garden with yellow
apricots after rain? One
treats oneself like a
suspect. One gathers
evidence: a stone that's thrown
must fall. You say
it was so long ago, but
I'm still here, a battlefield.
A tragic monument. One
offers one's beloved
an image, an assumption about
oneself to be transformed into
the beloved's image of the image.
Take me with you. I'm tottering
under the swan's weight

And caused us serious injuries
And that we must be those people
With ears that look like ass's ears
We lack someone in whose name we speak

What's the use of being a beautiful house by the railway

There's a door into the
dark, one gets used to it.
One gets used to everything: houses
and expensive clockwork. One can
sit on the steps and think about
trains that are leaving the great
stations in Europe. Gloves
left behind. The scent of phlox. There's
a rustling outside the circle of light: creatures
are passing. With love I
remember the untidy little towns with
optimistic names along the highway in the
purple evening across the prairie. Harsh sun
in motel rooms. The safety instructions
on the wall: 'If you are deaf, and your
travelling companion is blind...' I stopped
too long in the forest. I often call
the police, it's not worth calling
the police, that's the way it is.

Fever-free days along
the water, low clouds

The little bell is ringing
monotonously: How did

you live? What became of you?
In Chekhov there is a lot of talking

'through tears',
the cool scent of

snow, and that we must
endure everything. The heart

doesn't get damaged, the heart
is a lake where pictures

are reflected for a moment and
sink. As one looks at one's
most beloved pupil

Someone is still crying

Clouds, the cool
scent of snow

Why is the night so dark? Because
the universe is expanding.

I was sick.
I have won back my health.
That's why I wander from
door to door with the fearlessness
my Father restored to me.
The rain that streams along
the pane delights me now as before.
As in my youth I yearn
for the foreign lands.
The years went by and didn't leave
much to forget.
The little girl must have
endured, she ironed her
dress and walked to school.
We must endure knowing
nothing, we must endure
someone taking us in their arms and
killing us. I am well again.
That's why I stand on your
threshold now, wish you
nothing, good or ill.

What's the use of being a
beautiful house by the railway when
it's raining. When one gets confused with
anything at all, public buildings.
When on all sides there is nothing.
Before, there was forest. 'That is why it always
seems as though a peculiar veil of melancholy
were spread over plants and creatures: they are
all beautiful, they are all symbols of some
deep creative idea; but they do not know it, and
therefore they are sad.' Rooms for Travellers
to Rent. But if I stay there, what will happen
to me then? Unfurnished and those ugly radiators.
We long to make the world bright
and clear, as in Monteverdi.
But those empty floors. Dust, marks
of paws, felines.

You came to me last night in a dream,
and I don't know why I travelled about
so much that meanwhile I allowed myself to be robbed
of my possessions, everything. Nor why
I bought tickets to a host of unreal places,
and so what: how about certain people
taking a look at their own motives! I feel
ill, but no one seems to care about it. No one! You
stand once again beside my bed in the moonlit room,
that is bad, jawohl. I slowly undo the buttons
of my creased silk blouse, I undo
the buttons of my blouse, it's a clear, starry night and
I know: under tattered umbrellas we walk.

And caused ourselves serious injuries

Everyone is allowed here. You see again the
run-over creatures, and their little sister who
is you. Thin shapes cluster and look
at you childishly with eyes like moonlight. Roses
of blood come out on the bandages. You think
you recognise a gallant and cheerful little piece
you used to play. You see the horses again. There are
chilly avenues mirrored in cold water, but
one isn't cold.

The snow whirls over
Tenala churchyard

We light candles so that
the dead will be less

lonely, we believe they are
subject to the same laws

as ourselves. The lights twinkle restlessly:
perhaps the dead are longing for

company, we know nothing of
their doings, the snow whirls

The dead are silent as cotton.
A flock of thin children who

inaudibly take one step nearer
They look at us closely for a

moment: is it because they've
forgotten, or remember? The snow

whirls over Tenala churchyard

As when you fly in
over a city at night at

low altitude: the lights become
motorways, the headlamps of

the traffic, you arrive
from somewhere

Soon you are driving along a
road, one of the twinkling

lights in the whirling snow

But if we were nothing
but speed, then we couldn't
even travel anywhere.
I learned a lot in the forest.
I learned at least: that a
hunter is always a hunter. Stay
put, or run! There are
people who have specialised in
all kinds of things: eclipses of the sun or
flying through a thundercloud. With time
we get slower, our hands shake.
We're smitten with fever. I read a
letter that has travelled over a small
windy sea of archipelagos, and someone
lights the lamps in room after room.

And that the last pictures stay the same
With ears that look like ass's ears
What happens in the cylinder when the valve's position is altered
With lilies woven in her wonderful hair

We make such a pitiful
sight that the circus-master
is in tears. What is more, we're cold. Ach!
He wishes us to hell, he wishes
this muddy market-place in Ekenäs to
hell, with eyes closed he leaves
this slush-puddle for the continent, a
different place: where the ballerina's lace isn't
dirty, where the trapeze artist doesn't
smell of spirits, where the lion doesn't stare
despondently. Where cracks don't open
in the powder. Where cracks don't open
everywhere! The circus-master doesn't know
any such city, but it is painful to
grow old and remember without pain. Somewhere
the horses' coats are shining, spangles
glitter, the audience roars far away
from these bumpkins. There it is never
October with snow-mingled rain, there art
is memory and shimmering coins.

I dreamed that everything was
all right, that someone gave me the
black glove I'd lost,
that there were swans and a lot of
people. How matter changes
How we change when someone takes
us in their arms. Slowly, and you
stumble. For a while the heart is made of
glass. Evening like ash above the fields
'For one must be able to describe a
state where everything that can
be destroyed has been destroyed.'

And must be ferried through the night

We equip the horses with what
we lack: loyalty and
courage. We love them for their
loyalty and courage. It's November,
the wind blows gently in our faces, cold little
showers splash from the tree-
tops   The horses are frightened by their
imagination. The horses are frightened by
anything at all and set off.
Nature is not wasteful; nature follows
strict economic laws. The trees
stay put in the mist, motionless.
Something has slowly changed, I
know: what I remember doesn't
come back.

There was no assignment, there was
only the gale blowing over a heap of rubbish.
The special silence of the
dumping grounds. Music is not feelings but
pictures, memories of feelings, writes
Paul Hindemith. I think that is true.
Who wouldn't wish for a life full of
Zeppelins and happy garden parties!
What we do not know we must hold up to ridicule.
What we have ceased to love follows us.
I buy sea-green dresses
and hang them in my wardrobe.
It's pleasant in the big cities that
light up like starry skies in the evening.

I write to you because
there's a composure, that little
horse on Via del Corso which goes
where it doesn't dare: in the evening traffic
among harlequins, taxis and
make-up. It's raining. One recognises
oneself: the parks, something made of silver, rotten.
The stench. A bell's overtones at a distance
'We are permitted to be nothing. Like a river
we flow willingly into every shape'
Its unreality. Its everydayness, its
terrifying cleanliness. I'm setting off.
I'm going to a night conference.
I don't know what you are like, I don't
know what it's like, but it can't be like
this: sunshine in white rooms.

Everyone is allowed here

The elder flowers

The dead don't come to
fetch anything

They lack possessions

The snow whirls

Don't return parcels, haven't
forgotten anything

Cartilage, feathers

Patient waters

Patient flesh

Become garbage

Blown away over glass, inaccessible:

they must never again pass that
room where pearl necklaces break and the elk
loses his crown.

But someone had bought a boatload of withered flowers

I stopped too long
in the forest, it's important to appear,
not talk so much. Then one
might as well be the sort of wardrobe they
have in country hotels. One picks
something up and lets it go again. Muddle,
contradictions are all I see. Before, I
owned some books, a green room. And through
the darkness shines: I studied long
ago at a wonderful faculty. Near here
there's a lake that makes the passer-by
giddy, its surface seems to hover over the
low shore. It is painful not to remember
with pain any more. And I caught sight of
them, I saw for a moment how terrified
they were: the hunters at the edge of the night.

With ears that look like ass's ears
And someone had bought a boatload of withered flowers
So cheaply and sent them across the water
And smelt so sweetly there across the water:

Across the calm green water's surface
Drifting through the park in August
With white lilies shimmering around the pissoirs
With the stench, and feathers shining there

That bird never moves
in the daytime, you must have been
mistaken, you must have confused the beat
of its wings with the wind in the aspen's
foliage. It's easy to get attached to anything: a few
knick-knacks and poor shoes, a horse.
The Dark Companion follows us
The sense of defeat follows us
But on clear days I see the shore through
a pattern cut in tissue paper!
On clear days I don't see anything!
I don't know any more how you kill
time, after all, one must do something.
One must think that it means something.
Star-strewn houses, cloudy sky
It's as though someone were singing a
dark, monotonous song.

(Frightened, dragged through the muck)

Whose name is that you were no one,
Whose voice is that the silver flowed like silver
We lack someone in whose name we speak
And caused ourselves serious injuries
And caused ourselves serious rheumatic pain
And shreds of a cloth where
someone has embroidered clumsily:

I fly like an eagle to you
I swim like a fish
I hurry across the snow
on my strong paws

'In reality we never noticed that we were travelling. But in this way we got so far that in every place we believed ourselves to be *at home*.'

And so the party's over.
It starts to snow slowly and
wonderfully, the way I remember
it snowing on the white
house once. We must return
all that became our happiness, only not
its transformation into image. And its
transformations   It snows on rubbish
and streamers, it snows on
snow and candles in the snow that whirls like
giddiness. Gentle days, a little
stretch of water: In reality we
never noticed we were travelling.

After Spending a Night Among Horses

(1998)

translated by
STINA KATCHADOURIAN

Now the summer's gone
as if it never was.
It's still warm in the clearing.
But that's not enough.

Everything that could, came true
landed like a five-fingered leaf
straight into my hands.
But that's not enough.

Evil and goodness
Did not disappear in vain.
Everything burned brilliantly
But that's not enough.

Life took me under its wing,
saved and protected.
In truth, all went well for me.
But that's not enough.

The leaves didn't get burned,
the branches didn't get broken.
The day is washed clean like a window.
But that's not enough.

ARSENY TARKOVSKY

'Of course it's quite possible that I'm inventing this after the fact. But that time, he just came up to me and said: "Follow me", and I did. And I've never regretted that. Never.'

The snow whirls over the courtyard's roses

The snow whirls over the courtyard's roses.
Didn't bring my boots and scarf, leafing
through books, don't know what to do with all this light!
You wouldn't approve of the colours.
It's too striking, Andrei Arsenyevich, too
much, too much of everything!
You exchanged the wings for an aerial balloon, a clumsy
creation cobbled together from rope and rags, I remember so well.
Before, I had a lot and didn't remember. Difficult
to stick to the subject. Difficult to stick to the subject.
Hope to return. Hope to return to the principle
of wings. The fact remains: the freeze preserved
the rose garden last night. 'The zone is a zone, the zone is life,
and a person can either be ruined or survive when
she makes her way through this life. Whether she makes it or
not depends on her sense of self-esteem – ' A hare
almost hopped into the entrance hall here at the Foundation,
mottled against the snow; it's October in the hare's calendar.
You seem to be a moody sort of person
and it's possible that none of this is of interest to you.
On the other hand, you yourself complain fairly often.
I'm writing because you are dead and because I woke up
last spring in my streetside hotel room in Benidorm to that wonderful
high twittering. One shouldn't constantly say one is sorry, one should
not constantly give thanks, one should definitely give thanks. Lake
Mälaren like lead down there. The rest is white and red.

The angels in Karis

Walk around in shoes
too thin for February

on the railroad station in Karis
back and forth, smoking

Trains arrive and depart
Tomorrow will be just the same

Snow is falling lightly, glittering
Snow is falling lightly on their eyelashes

They breathe lightly like aluminium
They know about the god-forsaken places

They laugh! Nothing horrifies us as much
as when they laugh

Nothing horrifies us as much
as the godforsaken places

And whatever is red-rimmed

Never make friends with a crow

Never make friends with a crow!
a biologist said on the radio. A crow
gets attached to you easily, she'll tap on
the window constantly, a crow can easily become psychotic.
Nothing happens here. Nothing. Gardens
in the rain. Lemons in moonlight. A flock of jackdaws
flew up with a huge racket by the ruin last night. The bells
softly through the haze. The smoke, the ringing. Once I saw
the eyes of a little girl cloud over, it was irreparable
right from the start, it hurts. The cloud floated over the
violet eyeball, slowly in toward the
pupil, and then I could no longer
follow it, that cloud.

Summer passed so quickly

Summer passed so quickly, and I hardly remember
the house on the hill anymore. Still, I spent many
nights there. Lightnings illuminated the enormous magnolia.
A lightning bolt always takes the shortest way between a cloud
and the ground. The owner rarely showed up, not a leaf
moved in the wind. He was playing Kinderszenen on such a
precious instrument that you'd doubt the whole thing, afterwards.
I'm left standing with a glass key in my hand. Smoke, against
your face a dark gust. We easily consider ourselves
defeated. Deep down there the water is gleaming,
a tributary to the mighty Missouri.

'In Russia, it's common to have long, hopeless, persistent rains - - - Rain, fire, water, snow, snowstorms – everything belongs to the material environment that surrounds our lives'

Andrei Arsenyevich! You wouldn't like all this commerce!

This is how it was: You were supposed to walk around
all night, network, get in touch with
Los Angeles, the city without a centre
You were supposed to buy into virtual things,
'Amazing Arrangements' in the foyer of the Music Hall
You had to be lively and quick like a
dream in the morning hours
You had to be aflame with emotion
There would be no god-forsaken places
No one would be shattered there
There would always be a way out, Andrei
Arsenyevich. It would rain on the evil ones
and the good ones as it's always done.

PS

I mean, there would be
no difference
There would always be a way out
No one would be wasted
There would be no
seaweed deserts, no childhood,
no waterlogged forest.

The laughing jackass birds

Last night, a goods train raced through the house
We are hit by vertigo all the way into our sleep
We hurry, have to have time, we do everything to gain time!
A jackass bird cries out, and a laughing wave spreads from
bird to bird along the slope, a silvery string between
the trees under the southern Australian sky that
promises another day without shade.

I used to know a man

I used to know a man.
He said he was a doctor and
let his patients happily bleed to death.
He took walks during the nights
god knows where to, it wasn't to any
catastrophe-hit areas. I sat
in a rocking-chair, rocking. He played
the violin in a schrammelquartet and enjoyed it.
Whatever he did, he enjoyed it.
He said no one would want me.
I said no one would want him,
except me. I said I'll sell everything, it
won't cost anything. That man. His patients
really got so sick that they died.

Phone conversation

It's such a small ocean

The silence rushes through
the cable along the ocean floor,

an acoustic chamber
in a larger and greener

acoustic chamber
'Nothing has changed'

A small spider wanders on
the wallpaper and turns

There's a hiss on the line
like then, before everything

was digitalised
The fishes are noisy

It's so green

I also knew another man

I also knew another man.
He was an oceanographer, but I never
saw him go down to the shore. He said I was
sweet and that the eyes of the deep-sea fishes blacken
when they are about to make love, thus he won my heart.
He flew through the air to foreign lands and peoples.
I sat in a wicker chair, creaking.
He said no one would want me.
I said no one would take pity on him,
except me. When he came home he told stories
and we had fun. In my dreams he looked
like a stork. Oh that man. He belonged to the
great Storytellers, he told stories so well
that he believed every single word.

The swine

In the midst of all the beauty lifted out of its
underwater twilight he is a
Monster. Equal parts wild boar and man,
grinning sadly and terrifyingly. Female
visitors pass their hands over the hump on
the neck, matted and shining with grease
When someone transforms us, do we realise it?
Surrounding the Swine a watery world of clay, small coral animals
from the Cambrian, sea anemones, things that floated ashore

As usual the Commander sneaked away
The Commander, as usual, found a bed
and the rest of them ended up in the pig sty
The Swine is staring, horribly and shyly
We touch his neck, shyly:

Yes, it's his terrifying ugliness we are caressing
Yes, we shall be fired in high temperatures
Yes, we shall achieve a similar lustre
Rain shall fall on us and the swine
shall be restored to their real selves

Procris

You mistake someone for an animal and kill the animal
That's how it happens in the forest, that's all there is to it
I woke up from an eroded embrace and a dream
about how minerals should be stored: the sun won't
injure them, the moon won't injure them.
There was frost in the grass and the sea had frozen over.
Who writes the murky law?

Amber

I have an amber ring that
shimmers through the lake's water

I dive, stir up the silt, particles
of minerals loosen and float along

the bottom, just like the oak-blossom bud's
starry hairs floated and were enclosed in the stone

then, during the time of sabre-toothed tigers
and small horses

in the sub-tropical forests with elderberry
and camphor trees here, where we live in houses

You see more clearly underwater
You see more clearly when you are sick

I dive into the cool water, stir up
silt, particles float slowly, minerals

like the oak-blossom bud's starry hairs float
in amber through thirty million years, shimmering

in the lake's water when I dive, everything
is stirred up, gets cloudy, shimmers

'And if we hadn't had sorrow and misery in our lives nothing would have been better. It would have been worse. Because then there wouldn't have been any happiness either... And there would have been no hope. That's the way it is.'

On how long-term weightlessness
affects living creatures

The dogs in your films seem similar
to Laika. Did you too once stand
on a hill watching the tiny light travel
across the evening sky? If that dog had
a view, it would have seen the shining blue
globe with oceans and clouds. On the ground
they monitored Laika's breath. The satellite
crashed into the atmosphere and Laika fell,
falls in the rushing wind through black mirrors,
doesn't have to be airsick anymore, doesn't
have to eat when the bell rings. Laika no longer
travels in a hermetically closed cabin,
chained to instruments that show how
long-term weightlessness affects living
creatures. Laika travels in the darkness
pure of heart, along with all masterless dogs.
Laika's memory was honoured with a new
brand of cigarettes in the Soviet Union.
The first dog in space
didn't return, will
return as dust and rain.

Sextus Propertius

The Shades do have life: all things do not cease with death,
the pale ghosts escape the vanquished pyre.

Sorry it's taken me so long to answer, the summer passed so quickly.
Are there seasons where you are? Do you walk on sparkling and sharp
rocks? I think of you often. Tragic gestures, sunglasses,
careful deliberate steps... You know how it is. How all went wrong,
how stupid, how perhaps the wrong person finally went and died. All
bottoms fall out. All bottoms fall out. 'Terrible!' we shouted,
'terrible, fantastic!' Right now when I'm writing it's October with
snow in the air; saddle, bridle, disinfect wounds, state your ID number
and address, carry out necessary repair work on the south side.
Change to winter tyres. Whatever love is – no one found protection
against it. Are you together now? The clouds float slowly over the
fields, the wind is mild. I'd love to know how it ends. Is your
heart transparent like crystal? When we meet I'll
ask about those hyacinths.

The Fallen Donkey

I kindly ask you to take care of my house
I leave behind neither wife nor children
I leave behind arches and portals and animals
To the glory of God and because it is my craft

In the end, I chiseled out a fallen donkey
In May, I go to Germany and then back here
O Lord what will become of those of us
Who will not understand our frailty

Adam the stonecutter van Düren

It's beautiful in Sicily in the spring
when the lemon trees are in bloom

I'm writing because I attended
your concert, it was the sixteenth
of September. You played Prokofiev, and
it's strange about music: you return
to places that don't exist. Two questions
keep me busy. One has to do with
conditions and destiny. The other has to do with
Procris. That it occurred to her to run into the forest.
That she couldn't trust her mate! I visited a
museum of Renaissance painting and then, everywhere,
in the streets, in subways, I saw: light, silky blue and that
special tenderness. In everyone! In the animals! I teach at a
high school here. It's beautiful in Sicily in the spring when
the lemon trees are in bloom. Perhaps you prefer to travel
according to your own plans but I wanted to ask because music
restores us, and a cloud drifts in through the window into
my apartment as the clouds sweep by every
morning over the park where I walk.

September sixteenth

Night, blue. Night, black.
We so easily think ourselves lost.
But the bells on the small horse's
harness, and one day it'll be September sixteenth,
for all creatures and critters, for every tree!
The soul is shy. A little water and oats are enough
A few sparkling transparent rocks
It's not good to have decay that's far advanced and
to cry a lot or travel to meaningless
conferences, this we know, we who long
have lived in a severe climate.

Plumeria acutifolia

I walked in a city glittering
from exchange rates and low motels
Huge halls with slot machines
As if no one really lived there

Until, on a street corner among the car rental offices
Stood the tree as a cloud of scent and rain
Stood the tree as a cloud of scent and white flowers
That rained on me, sweet-scented and fell

It was a lukewarm and passing tropical downpour
The white flowers and the rain rained on me
I'm standing in soaked clothes and am old
And fragrance and rain surround the tree like a cloud

And there was no airline ticket to the northern hemisphere
I wanted nothing and wished for nothing more
And there was no deceit and no slaughterhouses
Only Plumeria acutifolia, in rain

Summer report
(for W.A.)

An area of high pressure has settled over Scandinavia.
There is a smell of smoke, but perhaps it's a mistake.
The Government is on summer vacation.
Are we going to have a common European currency?
Sophia is feeding baby squirrels, their mother was run over.
They already want to play and are climbing up Sophia's arms.
I'd love to have a lilac arbour, but
lilacs grow rather slowly, and everything right now feels
more temporary. I've saved my chocolate silver coin.
My little kitten ran away two months ago.
From a certain perspective it seems most natural disasters
nowadays are caused by human beings, don't you think?
What I observe here in the Finnish forest
you observed at some point in the Swedish forest,
that's the way it is this summer with many things!
A light still shines around Signe's hairdo.
The door to your room on Hornsgatan stood open.
In Australia the laughing jackass birds are laughing, in Scandinavia
there are no such birds, much is probably also due to
pure chance and you of course know all this.

'I don't know what would have happened with the film if the buckwheat hadn't been in bloom...How enormously important this was for me at the time. And then it actually bloomed!'

It usually doesn't snow in Central Sweden in October

Birgitta had placed some flowers in
the room in a glass, pale light violet against
the snow, tiny anemones with very thin
petals and clearly visible nerves. All is like before.
But we were unprepared for the snow, it normally
doesn't snow in central Sweden in October.
We don't feel well at all, Andrei Arsenyevich!
You probably don't appreciate my writing such things.
But we are lonely. And we are tired. And we are
deceitful. And we miss our parents.
There's a murmur behind the wall, insects
thudding against glass, is there a wish to ridicule us once again?
We fall ill, we forget. We burst easily into tears.
You know how it is, you know how we are, you find it
unacceptable. You think that enough is enough.
But I think that this establishment high up would
appeal to you, with the cool smell of chalk, cellar-vaults,
the bay as aluminium, the bells. The small island
that's called Africa. The overtones. The half-tones.
You have to start somewhere. But perhaps there is
no end, only waterlogged forest and the smoke from grass and
the swamps, Andrei Arsenyevitch.

Little Girl

1

Come here with a name that
we don't learn
Fell through ice blue
Blue shiny hair like water

2

'It's terrible to think about
death, Mummy. That it's dark
one doesn't see'

3

Come back
Came back anyway
The horses are running, it's
raining on the horses

The barber opened the shutters of his shop

The barber opened
the shutters of his shop.
I recognised the high bright
twittering, the willow-warblers. They examined
their cramped cages distrustfully, as if
they constantly were discovering the bars,
as if they were forgetting all the time. Many
people move to Benidorm in order
not to grow old. Because it's warm.
The willow-warblers twittered. I think they
were communicating with their flock. I wished
I was a robber-girl in a robber-band,
but I was standing on the street in Benidorm outside of
the barbershop in the sun.

The one who was there once

It's still snowing.
I walk up to the tower room and look once
more out over the bay: weight and dizziness.
Someone calls and offers optimistic
suggestions, and of course, one can dance the foxtrot
to the very last. But I prefer to make an excursion
to a nearby local museum or I'll sign up to join
the church choir as a mezzo-soprano, although I don't
sing very well. It's not easy. It's truly
problematic. I know which continent
you prefer, but right now there's an imbalance there between
the species: everyone took along some pet they didn't want to leave
behind. They eat each other now. I know what areas
you prefer, anyone who was there once always
longs to go back. The sweat and whatever things were crawling
on the walls when one went to bed. In the tropics the
ownerless dogs aren't ownerless in the same way,
they live and die. The snow whirls ever more violently over
the roses, the darkly shimmering remains of the night.
We don't remember everything, but quite a lot.

The city was sparkling

The city was sparkling at a distance, and
I stopped. Everything looked so beautiful,
the street plans and the terraced gardens,
as if water-transparent, and I saw it all
very clearly. I thought about the great cities
with cathedrals, and the small local museums in
the countryside in Sweden, and the meadow-sweet with its
strong fragrance, and I remembered how attached I had been
to the little kitten with the spotted paws who
ran away and how I had missed it.
I turned around and someone was crying, I couldn't
pay attention to it. The city was made of transparent glass.
I stood there. I saw my pre-eminent love.
Shimmering of pearls. The black swans. Chalcedony.
I tried calling the small kitten. Everything was sparkling.
I hesitated, I knew everything, I would
not come back.

The horses

After spending a night
among horses I remember the fresh

smell of ammonia and
melting snow, the green moon

over the green snow's crust, a rat
creaking in the hay room, how I shivered

in my overalls and wool cap toward
morning and how calmly the horses slept.

Minerals

(2003)

translated by
DAVID McDUFF

1

It's green the way it's green in May
It rains the way it rains in May when it's green
In the clear dream we know that we are dreaming
The horses run, it rains on the horses

2

One should keep one's minerals in a box
Dust wears out their durability
The brilliance that surrounds everything deserted
One must keep them dark

3

I dreamed I was too dirty to go
to a doctor in Grand Popo, Benin, West Africa.
The doctor turned my ears inside out. It
hurt. There are things that can't be buried
or dug up, one doesn't know what they are and there
are many rooms in the underworld and glitter from
spaceships that have crashed.

4

But somebody lift her then
quickly so her waist doesn't break
or the whole of her breaks
and just let her be

5

During the dark season
One must pass through many intermediary rooms
In a sprawling city with monuments
Greetings From A New Home

6

Digital silence is confusing. I know
an answering machine on which someone constantly holds their breath
and listens, forwarding one's dejected messages
to a secret intelligence service and from there to the Worst
Department where they carry the documents on silver trays
silver-happy in wonderful blue garments made of fabric.

7

It wasn't for what was useful
I'll take the one with the stained paws
A cloud of rain blows through the heart:
I was homeless and you took me home

8

It wasn't for the things
It wasn't for what was useful
It was for the frogbit and the slimed-up
lake, I remember the frogbit!

9

The one with the stained paws
We were children in the light green hazel wood
There are flowing grounds where currents meet and
whirl green and waves blow in different directions

10

There was a little crowd of us who went to the market in
Grand Popo every Saturday at ten, bright patterns children
and old folk goats dogs hens and fairly domesticated pigs.
In the middle Leena and I marched fair-complexioned and
really unnatural. Anyway we walked in the red dust and
the red mud in the hollows after cloudbursts God knows
how long ago forgotten and never have we laughed as we
did along the village street in Grand Popo when none
of us had any idea what it was all about.

11

Through the foliage of the chandelier
the sky with stars of gold above the pulpit:
'And you will ask me:
From how far away did you see me
when we were alive that time?'

12

Tunnel of smoke and cloud
Someone carried me in their arms I think
There were creatures there that did not leave me
It was dark. It went quickly

13
(old)

Apples thud silently to the ground
You will live in a single room
The radio destroys nearly all the characters
Mama I want to go home   All the time
at home now

NOTES & QUOTATIONS

The Parks

65: Egon Friedell: *Kulturgeschichte I*.
74: Ludwig Wittgenstein: *Philosophical Investigations*.
78: Hermann Hesse: *The Glass Bead Game*.
91: Friedrich Nietzsche: *The Gay Science*.

After Spending a Night Among Horses

95: based on Per-Arne Bodin's translation from the Russian.
97: from the wife's final monologue in Andrei Tarkovsky's film *Stalker*.
99: 'The zone is a zone...': from Andrei Tarkovsky's book *Sculpting in Time: Reflections on the Cinema*, trs Kitty Hunter-Blair (Austin: University of Texas Press, 1989).
103: from *Sculpting in Time*.
110: with reference to Åsa Hellman's sculpture, 'Touched by Circe'. [Trs.]
111: *Procris:* an Attic heroine/huntress known for her stormy marital relationship to Cephalus and for her willingness to be unfaithful. Procris accidentally killed Cephalus while spying on him in the forest. [Trs.]
113: from the wife's final monologue in *Stalker*.
115: Sextus Propertius was a Roman poet, born between 54 and 47 BC, best known as a Latin love poet who claimed that his life's occupation was love. His mistress was Cynthia. [Trs.]. This quotation is from Book IV, VII.
116: 'O Lord what will become...': Inscription under relief in Lund Cathedral.
121: from *Sculpting in Time*.

Minerals

134: 'And you will ask me...': from Gunnar Ekelöf: *Guide to the Underworld*.